THE UNTOLD LINES

PREFACE NOVEL

AF536479

THOMAS EDISON M.

Copyright © Thomas Edison M.
All Rights Reserved.

This book has been published with all efforts taken to make the material error-free after the consent of the author. However, the author and the publisher do not assume and hereby disclaim any liability to any party for any loss, damage, or disruption caused by errors or omissions, whether such errors or omissions result from negligence, accident, or any other cause.

While every effort has been made to avoid any mistake or omission, this publication is being sold on the condition and understanding that neither the author nor the publishers or printers would be liable in any manner to any person by reason of any mistake or omission in this publication or for any action taken or omitted to be taken or advice rendered or accepted on the basis of this work. For any defect in printing or binding the publishers will be liable only to replace the defective copy by another copy of this work then available.

To the God

to Readers

to Friends !!

Contents

Foreword

These were not all the words i wish i said. In fact most of these words i wish i *didn't* write.Just to the small fact of, i wish i didn't care… but sadly i do. But if i said the words i wish i did, then they wouldn't be my little secret, they would be words on paper in a book. They would be words taken out of context, because the world loves to take things out of context. The words i wish i said are between me and my party of a brain. because if you knew the words, then you would have such an advantage over me, and my quiet showers where i ramble on to myself about my words wouldn't be my secret anymore. You may be able to take most of me but you'll never be able to take all of me.

Preface

!

Warning:

This book addresses a lot of controversial subjects, and touchy topics.

so, to the close-minded people: there's your warning.

!

Acknowledgements

This is entirely up to you. Recognize whoever you feel contributed enough to your book that they deserve it. For example, common groups of people that Authors thank include:

Family members (spouse, children, parents) - Dad & Sisters

Friends - Who strived to get engaged in this book

Editors/people who worked on the book production - Self

Publishers - Independent

Coworkers/assistants - Nope & neva

Agents/managers - Nope

Contributors/advisers/sources of information - Some heartbroken guys

Teachers/mentors/bosses - Nope

Inspirations - Agatha Christie

Prologue

When I wrote my first book, Tom & his jerry, i never felt like it was finished. I wanted to add more, i had so much more to add. and my friends just said, why not write another book? i feel like there's so much in my mind, and so much poetry I'm constantly writing that i don't think i'll ever feel finished with simply one book. my book, Tom & his jerry was written mainly when i was fifteenth and sixteenth.I used to say to self 'Why the heck people ignoring my saying'. These are the words i try to hold back from saying. These are the words that could break things when they are the happy days. These are my thoughts tracked down almost every day. These are the words i wish i said. Not just to one person, but in general. Writing helps give me a voice, so these are the words i wish i could say, but i hold back. I'm living life on strings now. But the most beautiful words are the words you fear to say. The words you have trouble saying because you can feel them rather than voice them. The words that can't quite fit under a specific word, because these words are felt rather than said. These, well, these are the THE UNTOLD LINES.

enjoy.

- *Thomas edison .m*

- ***Edison***

- ***Green***

- ***Cast***

Chapters

1. Not letting abandon myself!!

This chapter is about saving yourself when no one else will. they can't hear the demons taunting you in your head and they can't feel your heart weeping through the silence.
sometimes the princess in the tower doesn't need a prince, sometimes the evil queen doesn't trap her up there. sometimes she
traps herself in the small, tall tower overlooking the Gray skies. and sometimes they won't hear her cry for help. this is the time where the little princess decides to save herself. sometimes she isn't even a princess, she's just a girl with a wandering mind. she can fight the demons herself and she can climb down herself. it takes time. but she can do it. This chapter is about not letting yourself abandon alone.

the fucking ghosts are

- *My sick backhealth*

i'm just taking my time
learning how to fly.
confidence is a
nightmare to insecure
edison.

he tried to fight for you but he didn't fight hard enough he didn't seem to sharpen his sword, instead he lost the battle and you were left in the castle

you don't need someone to save you from the tower

just *save yourself.*

There are more traitors in our AI based novel. Apart from jokes, Traitors are real and mouthwatery to blame.

02.09.2021 *use your words edison jealousy*

is a garment most worn under the layers of our soul because no

one will

ever

admit when

they're

jealous

.

i'm addicted to the feeling of adventure

. ***who am i to you?***

i'm scared to love, it's bad, i'm protecting myself so i'm so very sorry for you, trying to love

someone

broken like me.

it's not

you

it's me.

-rome in delhi

my

imaginary

friend would be happy to hear my adventures

but it's too bad he's left a long time ago. Btw thanks for you !!
- School hood
in time you will be fine.
[a statement to enhance ourself]
is it me?**it can only get better from here -**
positive thoughts

Ft.edison

i'm really really good
at lying i've been telling
people "i'm fine" now for 3 years it must suck that life is so painful to the ones
that try to enjoy it

- Logout >>edison

it's like i'm sitting in a crowd of
people on the bleachers,
but i still feel
like there's no one there

- empty they keep saying it will get

better but
when?
being
alone and feeling lonely are two different things
she is

blooming from the walls that she sits against no one else can
feel her presence but i can see it …

-the wallflower from my nation

fuck its imagination >>
Something that's sad is when you know someone's
falling in love with you but you're
sitting there afraid of falling for
them because you're not prepared to be hurt again. maybe i'm
the
madman
kinda
slender
the loudest silence is when everyone's left you and you don't
know why
- thoughts that haunt me god
dammit it happened to me :]
why is my mind so full of thoughts irrelevant to this? my
imagination is going wild and i'm trying
to pay Stop
attention to trying to
my math
homework. please everyone, Edison !!
sticks and stones may break my bones but
words
will *always* hurt me

Endura mass –
Replica BG

it's moments like this Hella bro if you regret this.

when you're in complete solitude

when you realize how lonely you really are

- *alone and lonely are two different things.* it's like i'm alone but i don't want anyone i'll push everyone away i can't deal with anyone i can't do it i don't wanna be here maybe someone will just sit with me in complete silence and maybe i'll be okay

let me take care of myself before i promise to take care of you. bravery is
when you
ignore the demons taunting you in
your head and you move on with your day.

i'd love to

seehow you see methrough youreyes.

i feelnumb, i
can't feelmyemotionsmybody myheart, iactlike it'stherelikei'm fine buthonestly myownbrain isconfusingme.

they all ask me

where do you see yourself in ten years?

i honestly don't know because a year ago i wouldn't see myself here. reflect now. i can't stand the judgmental looks they give me or the pity in their eyes just please stop worrying about me she jumped off the plank and dived in with the sharks little did they know a small weak girl like her had a heart
and the sharks in the water

were nothing compared to the ones swimming the the depths of her thoughts
- she lived

i'll keep writing you poetry even when my hands can barely move and you can't make out the handwriting if i "needed you" like you keep stating to everyone then how come i was alive

she gets broken only trying to give all her love you give too much of yourself to
you lose who you are.
full of depth and beauty but you were
afraid of the sharks how did i
stay

alive if i

didn't
even write? she's so delicate but her love burns so hard
them and
they'll end up wanting more, until way before you came
in my life and i was able to smile before i was told i was
beautiful i was
my soulmate before anyone else was i was an ocean
Humm'g to love songs by myse*lf*
i'm flying above watchingall on the ground weep
and i think, why be sad? there's a whole world out there then
i wake up and
i'm the one weeping on the ground
Where the fuck are you Rebecca?

you said you'd stand wid me till my breathe

i know what i

need so

stop telling me otherwise.

Spoiler alert:

She still lived without any guilt.

2. The unheard topics

This chapter is the one that is the most painful to organize. This chapter is for the love poems. The ones you wish you could erase, but they were true. And they were written on these sad pages. Sometimes you wish you could erase their face from your memories, because sometimes you think you'd be better off without their face replaying in your thoughts at night.

but you don't regret them, because when you look back on the memories you're reminded that there's someone that amazing out there. And maybe this time it didn't work, but maybe one day you'll find someone better for you. This is the chapter for the love poems you dread to look back on and refresh yourself on how much you miss them. and yes. you do miss them. and you're allowed to say that, even if they don't miss you.

i can't believe your cold hands can bring so much warmth to my heart.

i'm shivering walking to my car and you force me to take your jacket and you put it upon me thank you, for actually caring and pushing through my stubbornness

i

can't

believe i met someone like you even after what i've been through.

family can meananyone you'rewilling to fightfor.

you're my family now.

because
we'd all do
anything for you
anything
you need
we're always here for you.

you had a house built out of bricks and cement that only ended up being abandoned he built me a house with his own hands out of sticks and mud that is full of more life than any other house on the road.

- money isn't everything edison.

i fell in love with your mind and soul
before i fell in love with
what's
in your wallet and
your
pants.

true. your heart is almost
as empty as your promises. i'm not sure what
love is cause my mind has fooled me
before,
but
if this is what i
think
it is

then, i'm in love with you

i wish i couldfreeze timeand be in this ***moment with you all my life.*** with a tear *he whispers goodbye* and she sits there *watching the spark* leave his eye. Looping both of 'hem.

the nighttime is so fucked as I thought !!

She loves me…

(passion in eyes) She loves me not…

(emptiness in words) She loves me…

(drunken touch) She loves me not…

(scattered texts

She loves me…

(lips pressed) She

loves me not…

-the Lollipop

society's perspective on beauty isn't even based on a person's soul anymore it's based on their large ass and

tits.

so silent i feel

so calm just writing poems about you while you're asleep what ever happened to you and me?

betrayal. *verb* expose to danger by treacherously giving information to an enemy *i hope you learned a lot of lessons from me but*

i bet you didn't learn a thing. LOL

love letters on the floor oh i really wish you were knocking at my door

roses are

red violets are blue
and i think
i'm in love with you.
- Always

even if you broke my youheart into tiny
little
pieces, i'd still
never
talk shit about you.

i'm confused

you're nice to me to my face you're all sweet and lovely but as soon as i turn around
it's like you're
someone
different talking
to others about me.

- two faced

even after all that i can still look into your eyes and be unable to hold back a smile. i've tried every'tnk i love even harder over and over just hoping that one day you
will get off the top of my
list
but after
all this, i'm not sure
you'll want
me anymore.

my feelings haven't faded in fact they've grown it's sad to know
you've gone in a different
direction
murmers in deep silence a rebound to her
i'm not here cause i like
you i'm just kissing you because you're lips are convenient as
his are not here
it hurts
- when you're taken
for granted
we both thought we were on the same
page but it turns out we're reading
different stories

it's you it's always been you it will always
be you my imagination must be wild
if i still think you're loving
me
I think it's a over up fetish that I am carrying.
it's really all about who's the last one
on your mind
before you go
to sleep.
- it's always you

ican distract myself by watching movies i can distract myself by making films i can distract myself by listening to music or talking to new people or playing with my cats but what it really comes down to is what's on my mind when i'm sitting

all alone in my car and
usually it's you. we can't skip the hard part because it's gonna
help us grow you deserve more than the kind words i write about you on paper you deserve
the whole world wrapped
in tissue and a bow for just breath'g this air.
and being a glorioussight to see on this earth.
love. the little cafe before we went to lay on the beach the tidepools where we adventured
the place i call "lookout point" with my favorite view are all great places we've been
but my favorite place is anywhere with you. i stare into space when i'm with you you ask me what i'm thinking i'll smile and say nothing. let me let you in on a little secret.
i'm thinking of you i'm in love with you and my anxiety is making it hard for me to admit i'm sorry
you probably think something is wrong. but my mouth isn't allowing those three words out of my mouth oh boy,it's truei really dolove you.
everytime you say you love me it feels like the first time
those words came out of your mouth.
-it's never too much
i've almost finished putting the puzzle together the only missing piece is you.
24.12.2021

I'm ready whenever you're ready. I've set everything up perfectly for when you come back.
but for some reason, there's a voice in the back of my head, telling me you'll never love back, and you'll move on, i mean, after all, that's what all do. But hey, if it's different, i'm ready for you. **i'm always ready for you.**
Timeless eternity.
i'm writing so much about you, and i don't **ever** want you to see it. because i know it's not your fault and i know my words are harsh, it's mostly the scenarios that are being made up in my head about you

and i sure hope they don't end up becoming true.

what did i do?

- let me know so i can fix it

as soon as you show someone that you'd do anything for them then they may take that to their advantage. loving used to be so easy why is it so difficult now?
but why do we need a break if it was all okay before? we'll just end up exactly where we were.
why do you still walk near me
but act like i'm nothing you
are so dull now i want to saysomething but my lips can't make a sound. you turnedright into the words
you said you'd never be.
i still want to be with you even though your feelings aren't true.

I want you.

i love you.

maybe i did

something maybe you just realized maybe i hurt you maybe i'm the bad guy maybe you're better off without me

- maybes

stranger -> close -> stranger

i keep quietly thinking to myselfi can't wait to tell you about this but then

i realize you leftand i lost my bestfriend,Everything.

love is more than just a

four letter word.

you fall in love like how you catch your breath, slowly then all at once, and you don't realize you're in love until it leaves you once again. space is when the relationship isn't working space is when you're tired of fighting space is when you both need time space is when you can't heal together space isn't what i need space is what you say you need i guess we weren't on the same page.

the only thing coming out of your mouth is complete and utter bullshit.

*oh honey.*Other

girls

keep

falling for the

boys that believe love is just a word.

i wish i could stop writing but my words seem to sing their own tune you get over them like this- at first, you can't. his name is repeated over and

over inside your little brain, singing a tune to you.

until your heart gets bored of the tune that only ends up

breaking you. one day at a time, you get over

them when you stop searching for them in a crowd.

you get over them when every love song on the radio is just

another song. you get over them when every

place you went is just a new place to make memories in. one day

at a time. you get over them slowly, you get over them by focusing

on your friendships, you get over them by focusing on your

family. you get

over them by loving yourself. you get over them by yourself, not

latching onto a new one. you get over them when you realize

your worth is not another person.

you think you're over them, until you catch sight

of them in a crowded starbucks or sometime in your day, and you

can't explain why it hurt you, you thought you were over them.

until, you see them and all the memories

you had flushed your head and you remember how much you

miss them. one day at a time. you get

over them by doing everything else you love hoping

that their name will disappear from the top of that list. you get over them

when you realize they left you for a reason, and

maybe that reason means they won't come back. ever. you get

over them when you realize you both were reading different books but thought your page was the same.

fill in the missing halves

it's like you've killed all the butterflies in my stomach but i still love you.

- abuse or ignore it

just loving like i haven't been hurt you can't force or convince anyone to love you. they'll figure it out themselves. relationships are like building a house together there are little fights big fights agreements happiness and

when the house is finished that's like marriage, after it's done you

both will make minor renovations or large ones and you'll live in that house hopefully *for the rest ofyour lives*

i love you

- *wow.* i'm not mad i'm just hurt.

when you smile my heart just fills up with joy

my mind

is so

consumed

of thoughts of you and me and what we could've been if you didn't leave.

"they *always*come

back."

i see why

they call it

falling in love because

it's hard to catch yourself past a certain point and once you

fall it takes a fucking long time to pick yourself back up but
when you're in love you feel as if you're
flying soaring out of the cliff you fell down.
you may have broke my heart, but of course i'm so messed up,
i still want to show you i care. - You'll never know
i wanna cry with you but i can't because if i was with you i
wouldn't be able to hold back a smile.
i just have
to be the stronger person and hold my own
ground
against all these threats you're
throwing at me
you just
make my
lips form into this natural form and i
don't know how
- your smile
you
above all, you're the one
i never want to lose.
- the greatest single word poem ---
fuck the L word.
you said you
lostwho you were withme.
decision you make even if that means hurting me. *i still love you.*
is that my fault?

i support you and any *and leave the remains of their name out of that*
wonderfuli want you brainto want me
it's always easier said
than done, it's easier to
say you love someone
yet turn your back on them in their time of need but it's harder to
love them i never thought to
end this or this fast. you and i were
never
meant to be
even if we wanted to be

please please don't leave me they say that if it's meant to be then they'll
come back, i believ- e if they really loved you then they would never would leave.
love is when you run out of things to do, yet you never grow bored of one another
you grew bored
leave me if that's what you really want.

- it could still work.

every
tear out of my eye has your name on it.
i'll pretend i don't care because it seems to you
like i'm not there

please tell me

it will all be okay

to the girl i still love i'm sorry

16.01.2022 we all mess up, we're humans

sometimes i feel like i mess up beyond the boundaries of stupidity

all i know is that i follow my

gut instinct and it doesn't lead me in the best direction always…

sometimes i hope you put mayonnaise on your fries and your mind wanders to the thought of me.

sometimes i hope you see a clear blue sky and you remember my eyes lighting up for such a nice day. sometimes i wonder if you still remember my face in all the memories we had. sometimes i wish you were still here, but if you wanted to be then you would be.

you chose to leave, oh well.

not talking to

me

leads you nowhere

true love is fighting through the hardest of situations

- guess it wasn't true to you.

should ofstuck with mygut instinct*you always ask me*

what does the "look"

mean? "the look" means i

can't believe someone

as amazing as you

is spending their time with someone like me

"the look" means i look at

you and can see youas the only person in the world

"the look" is when i can't describe in wordshow

much i love you.

how'd i end up so lonely again? don't give up on me i could be what you need ***you're a walkingmasterpiece***so many constant thoughts in my mind constantly hurting me repeating the words you told it

we're sitting in a field of dandelio ns and grass just watching the time tick away and pass

i keep on having this recurring dream, that i see you in the distance and naturally i start walking to you. and as i get closer and closer i make eye

contact with you and i fall down, this deep hole... then i wake up. the last image in my head in the morning is you watching me fall so helplessly down

this hole, screaming and shouting. and you watch my with no expression, and no sense to help me.

- maybe it foreshadowed something?

if it was easy to move on then it wouldn't be love would it? i wrote you two love poems yesterday i wrapped them together, put a bow around them and i was going to hide them somewhere you'd find.

the hope from yesterday made me so inspired, i thought i'd do something for you this morning was my first heartbreak you've given me, i say first because even in the slight chance you come back, i know i won't refuse *i need you* even as a

friend
i don't need time to myself please see
that

- a tragedy

This heartbreak will be nothing like the others
because this heartbreak is something that i know you
wouldn't have
chosen.

- sucks

i just wanted to let you know, i'm *always* here for you, whenever you need me please just dm me, and i'll answer, even if you just want to talk about your day or something silly
i'm here for you
and i'm not leaving
anytime soon (unless you want me to) i'll never stop loving you

"i'll never hurt
you" "i'll
never leave
you"

- top two biggest lies even if it's not intentional i hate it. i hate still being in love with you
i know it's not your fault

and i really do wish i was still in your arms
but hey maybe one day it will work maybe time is what we need
i'd still do
anything
for you
but i don't know if you want
me
to
i'd still
fight for you but i don't know if you want me to
black and white but that's not life

- the grey area do you ever love someone so much that you only want the best for them?

then you come to the realization that maybe you aren't the best for them.

- most heartbreaking conclusion they

>> say if you love something,
then set it free but why has that made us both unhappy?
now you're just a stranger with all my secrets and dreams
i thought i was okay
if something breaks
your heart, then why do you keep watching?

"because we're hoping for a different outcome."

until i saw your face i'm not the boy that a girl will chase from side of the world to the other. i'm not the boy that all the girls praise and describe her with words like "perfect". i'm not the boy girls would wait a lifetime for. i'm not the boy you'd see in a romance movie that doesn't have a sharp bone existing in their body. i'm not the boy they'll follow all the way to the airport to say goodbye to. i'm not the boy they'll stand outside the window with a radio for. i'm not the boy they'll ever need. i'm just the boy they'll waste their days with until the right one comes around. i'm just the boy they'll leave

when things

get hard. i'm just the boy to

pass their time. they say they'll never leave you until they do even if they don't want to they think they know what's best for you

- charmastic of a boy >> rather be edison

for the girl i still love, i've written more poetry about you and you wouldn't have a

clue the fact that i still love you more than you ever knew.

my heart isn't messed up by

your thought but by the memories in my mind your face your touch your smile *oh god that smile.* the one i could stare at all night and all day i've never gotten over you because i've never felt the need to just the thought of you makes me sing a tune just a picture makes me smile even though it should make me die a little *just you.*

the thought that we could still be what we once were just the *hope* in my eyes that one day i'll have you back.

but what kills me is that i can't reserve you because you're not a library book or a table at a crowded restaurant and worst of all, you're not mine, anymore.

"it wasn't us" i keep telling

myself "it wasn't me" i keep telling

myself "it was the timing" i keep telling myself

yet my messed up mind will tell me that you could find someone to love you more that no matter how many times you told me i was perfect i knew you could find someone else i may love you more than words can describe and that won't ever let me stop thinking about you at night i've written so much poetry about you and you wouldn't have a clue.

i thought

you'd be my everything but you only our hearts left me with both broke nothing. different ways, sadly…

now out broken

pieces don't fit together like a puzzle

sorry if

that was too much

-

we have to find our missing piece elsewhere.

Spoiler alert: as much as she wanted him she never *needed* him

3. The unbloomed sides.

Beware:

This chapter is for the mentally fit beings. The pages people don't dare write about. These are the pages that make me different. because i'm not hiding them in the shadows anymore. I've written these but i've never shown them to a soul. This is the time i'm showing them. the best advice i've gotten is write about what you're most scared to say. here's what i'm scared to say. i'm scared about the people that will perceive me different after reading these. that will show their pity in their eyes. *i don't want your pity.* these are the pages that no one talks about. a trigger warning: these pages may get too much at times, these pages are here to show you that these are real feelings and thoughts. if you are feelings suicidal please find help, or call the hotline. and please please understand that you are not alone. you're never alone. even though out of the 7 billion on the planet you feel like you're suffering in silence, you aren't. **enjoy the darker pages.**

national suicide prevention hotline: 1-800-273-8255

entry: 28.01.22 one of the darker days

I don't think i've felt this alone for a while. I woke up this morning, three hours before my alarm, hoping, praying that nothing happened. that i would wake up on tuesday, february sixth and realize it was all just a nightmare. but it wasn't. That was reality. I'm a stupid teenager. I may even be a slut, who knows? but why does *my life* have to follow a plan? why am i treated like a puppet? why am i not good enough in their eyes? my mind is common to overthinking.. my mind is prone to insanity. The cuts i lay upon my Knee and arms aren't even a little pain that i'm feeling in my head. Most times i wonder why i haven't killed myself yet. I was so happy but now i'm so so very sad. I don't think my happiness ever stays long, i don't think it will ever stay long. the sadness always comes back to haunt our minds.

the pain will never go away *{ the sadness lasts forever }*Sometimes i wonder why people look at death like it's a tragedy. it's not the tragedy, it's everything leading up to it that is the tragedy.

maybe we're the bad guys

i don't know what hurts more my heart or my brain?

-confusion take a gunto my headbecause i'd bebetter off dead.

i wish i could take a

knife and end my life.

okay i've had

my fun

- suicide

even the happiest of times are just false reality

maybe if i justkill myself thenyou can stopworrying aboutme.

hurts like hell.

- missing you

;

to clarify why the last page was a single semicolon. a semicolon is when an author could've chosen to end their sentence, but they did not.

let it sink in edison

you know i was in love with you right?
"and what changed?" nothi ng. may
be
insanity is
underrated

.

i'm strong you've never seen me
weep
even after all this and that's because as soon as you walk away i'll be weeping harder than you'll ever know, but i'm strong enough to hold it in so it will never hurt you. let me eat enough food so i can drown in
my sorrows

taunt my corpse

- *they'll never learn*

i'll be
okayjust maybe not
today

grades are more
important than
my mentality

2:45 PM

I'm not perfect and

I never will be unrequited Solitude is the one that fucks us all up.

my hearts thrown in

the gutter dragons are the *again.*boys that promise you everything but leave you with nothing

i'm making promises to you and you won't even see.

It's hell being twentieth.

i would die

for you if you want me to i would fight for you if you want me to i would lie for you if you want me to

it's been Three years and i

but would

that all be the same for you?

still don't

want to be here

the untold lines.

Its be your untold lines>>

Let me grab your sick heartbroken quotes into my next book

CHAP : 02

Mail is given on the last page Spam readers !!

silently screaming. i just want her

she's the only thing on my mind

even if i try to think of anything else

my mind wanders back to the

thought of her.i'm starting to think i'm going insane and to escape the thoughts of him are only if i blow my fucking brains out. *twinkle twinkle little star let me get hit by a car jump off a roof and try to fly oh god i wish i could die twinkle twinkle little knife help me end this wretched life.*

don't you fucking mind?

i keep letting them hurt me and i'm doing nothing to stop it.
you're killing me with
all the silence. i carve lines and act like i'm fine. how
selfish would i
be if i just
decided to leave?

why me?

hey hey hey
guess what i'm a human being too!! they ask me how i am
i say i'm tired but they aren'
asking me what i'm tired of.

sometimes i wonder who i am… well most times. i've become so accustomed to wearing masks around different people and faking a smile with so much pain… that, i ask myself: who? am? i? i have to take that step back, evaluate, and decide. what makes me… me? what qualities do i have? how do other perceive me? i end up getting to the conclusion to stop getting in my own head and being silly. to sit back and relax. but i'm one of the rare few that has so much trouble relaxing. my mind wanders…. i'm a dreamer they say. i think too in depth. oh well. undeveloped
polaroids unspoken words untouched
hearts unmarked maps unclear messages
- path to a broken soul

she's sick sick of all the lies sick of being let down sick of putting her all into something that just hurts her more
she's sick
her smileshinesbrightbecause she doesn'twant anyoneto see thepain under it

i'm sick

of choosing which mask
i'll wear each day
because i'm afraid of showing my true self to the ones who will try to take advantage of it.

Spoiler alert:

She lets out a smile.

4. Out of imagination.

This chapter is about the realizations you make after an incident. when you thought everything was great until you look deeper into it. yes. These are some words i wish i *didn't* write. but that's what they are. you don't ever want the harsh realizations, you always want the sugarcoat. but once again, these are the words i'm afraid to write. these are the realizations that sometimes haunt me at night. these are the poems that hurt to look back on. in fact, these are the words i *didn't* say. since when i wrote them they were my "mind overthinking" but they became true. not every single one. just some. but still. wow. didn't think i could predict the future that well. enjoy this chapter of **Imagination.**

my mind is gonna
explode
with allthe thoughts ofwhat we could'vebeen.

10:55 PMmissing you usually comes in showers
tonight is a thunderstorm talk to me
didn't know i was so disposable he is the poem i wouldn't dare
to write i
would push through, scared, to see the words i
chose because he was the one i was madly in love with even if
i wouldn't
admit it.

i can't be your hero
you think it's all a
game and
i'm your favorite card to play.
i hate to
say it but sometime s
i feel like i didn't
exist in your life because you loved
me i feel like i exist in your life for the attention you crave and
the gap of loneliness to fade
i don't hate you i just hate that i can't have you
you only loved me when i was weak because it made you feel
better about yourself. i'll never
hate you
even if i act like i do.
he was the whirlwind that swept me off my feet
but only ended up leaving me to weep.
"how'd you know it was over"when his eyes stopped lighting up. I tried drinking i tried driving 100 on the freeway i tried extreme sports but nothing will be the same as when my heart was next to yours

The only thing that's your fault is making me fall
so goddamn head over heels for you. their opinions are only attempting to burn through the pages of love story but , *they haven't seen the pages that are far from flammable.*
why were you able to move on so quickly if i was the one you
loved? why am i always the one left abandon?

I am probably more in love with the
memories than the person i created them with. i can't
believe this but i'm used to getting what's unexpected.

Spoiler alert:

Sometimes realizations and overthinking become your best friend. Sometimes it helps you predict what's going to happen before it does. Even though, you hope that they'll never happen, they still do.

Sometimes as much as you hate overthinking, you won't be caught off guard.

5. Queries of this world ??

This chapter is about the questions of this world. Since the other chapters were about your own world in you head, i thought, why not make one about the actual world. either made up. or living. sometimes i don't like this world, and i don't understand it. so i make up my own. and it's easy because i can make up my own rules and my own thoughts. and all the negative people are out of it. My world inside my head is wild, but if i ramble on about it it will be the size of another book. (maybe i should write one). This chapter is about the messed up beautiful world we live in. And it's about the world up in our brains.

it's fucking terrible to love someone but live in fear that they're going to leave or hurt you. we'll break someone else's heart before they break ours.

because we're scared we don't want to be the one hurt,or broken we'd rather be the asshole that dumped someone.what a fucking cruel world.

i don't like the it loses it's power to recover the
world ashes of the heart so i made up
my own
after time, sorry loses it's value that it once had
the world relies so much on money, and
material items i get essentials but.. the five

thousand dress i get from goodwill is just as good as the fifty thousand dress you buy somewhere else. *it's just fabric* my car works just fine. would i like a new one? yeah probably. *do i need a new one?* no.

it's just an object. it's just material. adventures and experiences are *wayy better* than those twenty thousand rupee gucci slippers you "need" flying to see your family is way better than your 5 crore lamborghini yeah, cool car, we get it, you have money grow up, stop basing life on materials and *live a goddamn life.*

03/02/2022 i saw a tweet the other day that said *"break her heart and she's yours forever"*

the point of this frustrated me so much. it clearly shows how some people only truly date for attention. it's disgusting how you can even ***want*** to break someone's heart. they invest time into your crusty ass and you're over here sending tweets about breaking their heart. *you attention seeking whore.*

love is about building each other. not breaking one for attention. humankind is now so absorbed in their phones like hi?

i'm right here, a human

to talk to right in front of you the reason why

relationships don't last nowadays is that when the "spark" is gone, they find it boring. the start of relationships are almost always fun. but *real* love is sticking there with the person through all the ups

and downs, through the good and bad. real love is

loving someone through their best and through
their worst.
real love is building each other up. real love is staying there even when the "spark" is gone.
i may not know much about "love" because i'm some stupid adolescent but if i know anything about love
it's that you'll stay no matter what.
if you voice your thoughts and emotions and he fears it then he has no reason to hear it what if what is isn't what is isn't what's impossible is possible what's possible is impossible and what's imagination is reality and what if mere reality is just our imagination

23.07.2017

coach put me in i
need to

run
and we may not win but
isn't it all about the fun?

almost all children had an imaginary friend i didn't.
i had an imaginary "monster" i eventually became comfortable with fearing it and dealing with the pain it caused and eventually i became comfortable of being attached to it i guess that's why i'm so attracted to boys with empty
hearts that
make empty promises because i've
became so
accustome

d to dealing with pain.
learn the

most from
the ones
we hate the
most *what*
if my green
is your blue

- sorry

there's a difference

between living and existing

Spoiler alert:

These were not all the words i wish i said. In fact most of these words i wish i *didn't* write.Just to the small fact of, i wish i didn't care… but sadly i do. But if i said the words i wish i did, then they wouldn't be my little secret, they would be words on paper in a book. They would be words taken out of context, because the world loves to take things out of context. The words i wish i said are between me and my party of a brain. because if you knew the words, then you would have such an advantage over me, and my quiet showers where i ramble on to myself about my words wouldn't be my secret anymore. You may be able to take most of me but you'll never be able to take all of me.

Authors Note:

Thank you for reading yet another one of my books written from my partying brain and weeping heart. I hope you enjoyed it, and i hope you were able to relate to some of it. Writing is a safeplace and it's easier to write things in condensed little words on paper rather than voice them to chatty humans. if you enjoyed this, let me know, I love to hear feedback and your own quotes too. Mail your feedback and quotes to michaelthomas0063@gmail.com Waiting for your feedback !! *thank you.*

9 798886 418613

Printed by Libri Plureos GmbH in Hamburg, Germany